Expository Nuggets
from
Psalms and Proverbs

Mark & Debbie Stuenzi
208 Maple Avenue
Clarks Summit, PA
18411

Expository Nuggets *from* Psalms and Proverbs

Stuart Briscoe Expository Outlines

D. Stuart Briscoe

Baker Books

A Division of Baker Book House Co
Grand Rapids, Michigan 49516

© 1994 by D. Stuart Briscoe

Published by Baker Books
a division of Baker Book House Company
P.O. Box 6287, Grand Rapids, MI 49516-6287

Printed in the United States of America

ISBN 0-8010-1089-6

Contents

Part 3: Sound Sense for Successful Living

Preface

Outlines and skeletons are quite similar. Sermons without outlines tend to "flop around" like bodies without bones. But bones without flesh are not particularly attractive; neither are outlines without development. The outlines presented in this book are nothing more than skeletal for a very good reason. I have no desire to produce ready-made sermons for pastors who need to develop their own, but on the other hand I recognize that many busy pastors who find sermon preparation time hard to come by may at least use them as a foundation for their own study, meditation, and preaching. They can add flesh to the bones; they can add development to structure. All the sermons based on these outlines have been preached during the last twenty-two years of my ministry at Elmbrook Church in Milwaukee, Wisconsin, and as one might expect, they vary in style and substance—not to mention quality! I trust, however, that they all seek to teach the Word and apply it to the culture to which they were preached, and if they help another generation of preachers as they "preach the Word" I will be grateful.

Part 1

The Pursuit of Happiness

1

There's More to Happiness than Having Fun

Psalm 1

Everybody wants to be happy. Opportunities to be happy abound. The Declaration of Independence guarantees Americans the freedom to pursue happiness. But what exactly is happiness?

- I. The problem with happiness
    - A. It's so elusive
        1. Free to pursue it
        2. Pursuing where it isn't
    - B. It's so ephemeral
        1. I think I've found it
        2. But I might have lost it
    - C. It's so expensive
        1. Happiness depending on happenings
        2. Happenings are such a burden

II. The principles of happiness (vv. 1–2)
   A. It is not found in godlessness
      1. Godlessness produces meaninglessness
      2. Sinfulness produces guiltiness
      3. Skepticism produces bitterness
   B. It is related to godliness
      1. The Lord
      2. The law of the Lord
      3. The love of the law of the Lord
      4. The lifestyle of the love of the law of the Lord

III. The profile of happiness (vv. 3–6)
   A. The godly are like trees
      1. Stability
      2. Sufficiency
      3. Productivity
      4. Reliability
      5. Prosperity
      6. Serenity
   B. The godless are like chaff
      1. Without substance when the winds come
      2. Without excuse when the judgment comes
      3. Without hope when the kingdom comes

2

How to Be Happy in a Crazy World

Psalm 2

The psalmist was aware of his world and asked good questions about it. He found answers in the Lord; so, too, must we.

I. Evaluate the world situation (vv. 1–3)
   A. The conditions (v. 1)
      1. International conflict (heathen rage—literally "nations in tumult")
      2. Individual confusion (vain thing—literally "emptiness")
   B. The causes (vv. 2–3)
      1. The arrogance of the leadership
        a. Self-sufficient
        b. Self-confident
      2. The antagonism to the Lord
        a. Jehovah
        b. Christ

3. The attraction to liberty
   a. Break the bands
   b. Cut the cords

II. Recognize divine superiority (vv. 4–9)
   A. The superiority of Jehovah
      1. God's will is sovereign (v. 4)
         a. He laughs at fallibility and mortality
         b. He derides rebellion
      2. God's word is sure (v. 5)
         a. Authority
         b. Judgment
      3. God's way is settled (v. 6)
         a. My king
         b. My hill
   B. The superiority of Messiah
      1. Sonship declared by resurrection (v. 7; see also Acts 13:33; Rom. 1:4)
      2. Sonship deserving rights (v. 8)
      3. Sonship demonstrated by rule (v. 9)

III. Engage in productive ministry (vv. 10–12)
   A. Exercise your mind (v. 10)
      1. In light of his inevitable triumph
      2. In light of his invincible purpose
   B. Exert your will (v. 11)
      1. Submit with reverence
      2. Rejoice with respect
   C. Express your feelings
      1. Because of God's dislike of secret discipleship
      2. Because of God's display of spiritual blessings

4

Happiness and Discouragement

Psalm 11

In this world, as in David's world, there is much to be discouraged about. This is undeniable and unavoidable. So what can be done about it?

I. David's discouragement (vv. 1–3)
    A. Discouragement born in adversity
        1. Bending of bows
        2. Shooting from shadows
        3. Crumbling of foundations
    B. Discouragement nurtured by advice
        1. Look out for yourself
        2. Abandon hope and "flee"

II. David's declaration (v. 1)
    A. A declaration of dependence
        1. I take refuge–the need for security
        2. I lean upon–the need for support (Ps. 9:10)
        3. I roll on–the need for significance (Ps. 22:8)

B. A declaration of indignation
   1. How can you think what you're thinking?
   2. Don't counsel me the way that you're counseling!

III. David's delight (vv. 4–7)
   A. He delights in who the Lord is
      1. He is righteous
      2. He loves justice
   B. He delights in what the Lord is doing
      1. He intercedes as Priest
      2. He reigns as King
      3. He watches as Father
      4. He evaluates as Judge
   C. He delights in what the Lord will do
      1. He is promising eternal salvation
      2. He is committed to ultimate victory

6

Happiness in the Shadow of Death

Psalm 23

Life is lived in death's shadow. The longer we live, the longer the shadow. This thought can be so paralyzing that man's ingenuity has been stretched to cope with it. The psalmist, himself no stranger to the valley, shows the best way.

I. Life and death's shadow
   A. Living life in the light of death
   B. Approaching death in the light of life

II. Life with David's Shepherd
   A. A Shepherd who brings enrichment (v. 1)
   B. A Shepherd who provides fulfillment (v. 2a)
   C. A Shepherd who leads to contentment (v. 2b)
   D. A Shepherd who offers refreshment (v. 3a)
   E. A Shepherd who gives government (v. 3b)
   F. A Shepherd who imparts encouragement (v. 4)
   G. A Shepherd who prepares armament (v. 5a)

    H. A Shepherd who pours out enduement (v. 5b)
     I. A Shepherd who produces enjoyment (v. 5c)
     J. A Shepherd who guarantees equipment (v. 6a)

III. Life in divine secret
    A. A powerful relationship–"The Lord"
    B. A practical relationship–"Shepherd"
    C. A positive relationship–"is"
    D. A personal relationship–"my"

8

Forgiven People Are Happy People

Psalm 32

Saint Augustine said, "The beginning of knowledge is to know oneself to be a sinner." The next step is to know what to do about it. David knew and wrote about it in Psalm 32.

I. An explanation (vv. 1–5)
   A. Explanation by way of instruction (vv. 1–2)
      1. Blessedness comes from the forgiveness of transgressions
         a. Forgiven–lifting the burden
         b. Forgiven–"sending away" the guilt
      2. Blessedness comes from the covering of sins
         a. Sins–failing to do what is required (Judg. 20:16)
         b. Covering–out of sight (Isa. 38:17; 43:25; 44:22)
      3. Blessedness comes from the canceling of indebtedness

   a. Iniquity—distortion, absence of respect
   b. Not counted—accountability canceled
  4. Blessedness comes through spirit without guile
   a. Spiritual exercise
   b. Genuine, wholehearted
 B. Explanation by way of illustration (vv. 3–5)
  1. The experience of an unrepentant spirit (vv. 3–4)
   a. A sense of weariness (v. 3)
   b. A sense of heaviness (v. 4a)
   c. A sense of emptiness (v. 4b)
  2. The experience of a repentant attitude (v. 5)
   a. Cover-up ended
   b. Confession made
   c. Consciousness of forgiveness

II. An exhortation (vv. 6–10)
 A. Pray at the appropriate time (vv. 6–7)
  1. High above the floods
  2. Hidden among the troubles
  3. Happy amidst the conflict
 B. Follow an appropriate path (v. 8)
  1. A new way of life
  2. A promise of direction
 C. Behave in an appropriate manner (v. 9)
  1. To be mulish is to be foolish
  2. To be submissive is to be smart
 D. Adopt an appropriate stance (v. 10)
  1. The options are obvious
  2. The decision is decisive

III. An exclamation (v. 11)
 A. Those who understand sin understand repentance
 B. Those who understand repentance understand forgiveness
 C. Those who understand forgiveness understand praise

9

When Frustrations Get in the Way

Psalm 37

We live outward and inward lives. If we allow the outward to dominate, the inward suffers. If we nurture the inward, the outward is changed. Which way we live determines whether we are happy or frustrated.

I. The frustrations we face
   A. God seems to be unfair
      1. The godless have it easy
         a. They do enviable things (v. 1)
         b. They enjoy remarkable success (v. 7)
         c. They live charmed lives (v. 21a)
         d. They escape unscathed (v. 32)
         e. They get all the breaks (v. 35)
      2. The godly have it so hard
         a. They have to live differently
            (1) Do good (v. 3)
            (2) Be just (v. 6)
            (3) Be meek (v. 11)

   (4) Have little (v. 16)
   (5) Be blameless (v. 18)
   (6) Give generously (v. 21)
   (7) Be faithful (v. 28)
  b. They have to take their lumps
   (1) The opposition they face (vv. 12–14)
   (2) The reactions they can't make (see A.2.a.)

 B. Desires go unfulfilled (v. 4)
  1. They desire like anyone else
  2. The desires are often denied or delayed
 C. Life is never straightforward
  1. The way is full of stumbling blocks (v. 24)
  2. The slope is always slippery (v. 31)

II. The lessons we learn
 A. God will inevitably triumph (vv. 18–20)
 B. God will eventually prevail (vv. 9–15)
 C. Godliness will ultimately satisfy (vv. 37–40)
 D. Grace will continually flow (vv. 23–25)

III. The disciplines we develop
 A. Disciplined attitudes
  1. Trust and do (v. 3a)
  2. Dwell and enjoy (v. 3b)
  3. Delight and desire (v. 4)
  4. Commit and trust (v. 5)
  5. Be still and wait (v. 7)
  6. Wait and keep (v. 34)
 B. Disciplined reactions
  1. Don't get frustrated (vv. 1, 7, 8)
  2. Don't get mean (v. 21)
  3. Don't get careless (v. 27)
  4. Don't get discouraged (v. 37)

11

The Joy of Sharing

Psalm 45

This wedding song was written for a festive occasion, but was apparently intended for use by succeeding generations (see v. 17). This fact, coupled with the application of the psalm to Christ (see Heb. 1:8–9), allows us to apply its exuberant message today.

I. The joy of sharing (Ps. 45:1, 17)
- A. The exposure to a noble theme
- B. The exuberance of a stirred heart
- C. The experience of a responsive person
- D. The expertise of a practiced tongue

II. The sharing of joy (vv. 2–16)
- A. Joyous appreciation of the Bridegroom (vv. 2–9)
  1. The Bridegroom's humanity (v. 2)
     - a. The graciousness of his lips
     - b. The excellence of his character

2. The Bridegroom's majesty (vv. 3–5)
   a. Dressing in glorious splendor
   b. Riding in victorious humility
   c. Engaging in wondrous deeds
   d. Overcoming in momentous fashion
3. The Bridegroom's deity (vv. 6–7)
   a. God of the eternal throne
   b. God of the righteous scepter
   c. God of the joyous anointing
   d. God of the loving heart
B. Joyous appreciation of the bride (vv. 10–16; cf. Eph. 5:23–32; Rev. 19:6–10)
   1. A responsive bride (v. 10)
   2. A resplendent bride (v. 11a)
   3. A respectful bride (v. 11b)
   4. A respected bride (v. 12)
   5. A rejoicing bride (vv. 13–15)
   6. A resourceful bride (v. 16)

III. The job of sharing
   A. The sharing of worship
   B. The sharing of nurture
   C. The sharing of mission

12

When You've Lost Your Joy

Psalm 51

David's experience with Bathsheba and the resultant consequences constitute a desperate low point in his life. That he lost his joy is understandable. That he recovered it is reassuring and encouraging. What do we need to do in similar circumstances?

I. We need to find the reasons (2 Sam. 12:1–14)
   A. David had pursued happiness in self-indulgence
      1. Successfulness led to laziness
      2. Laziness led to selfishness
      3. Selfishness led to wantonness
      4. Wantonness led to willfulness
      5. Willfulness led to sinfulness
   B. David had pursued happiness in self-delusion
      1. He would not be caught–but he was
      2. He would not be accountable–but he was
      3. He could handle the situation–but he couldn't

        4. He would not hurt anyone–but he did
        5. He would not be exposed–but he was
    C. David had pursued happiness into a corner
        1. He reaped what he sowed
        2. Others reaped what they didn't sow
        3. Some reaped more than they sowed

II. We need to face the facts (Ps. 51)
    A. The fact of sin
        1. Sin as a propensity (v. 5)
        2. Sin as an activity (vv. 2–4)
        3. Sin and accountability (v. 4)
    B. The fact of confession
        1. Confession of what I am (vv. 5–6)
        2. Confession of what I've done (vv. 2–3)
        3. Contrition for what I've demonstrated (v. 4)
    C. The fact of mercy
        1. Merciful attitude expressed by God (v. 1)
        2. Merciful actions performed by God (vv. 7–9)
    D. The fact of restoration
        1. A new heart created (v. 10)
        2. A new spirit granted (vv. 10, 12)
        3. A new assurance experienced (v. 11)
        4. A new joy displayed (v. 12)
        5. A new ministry envisioned (v. 13)
        6. A new worship enjoyed (vv. 14–16)
        7. A new attitude developed (v. 17)
        8. A new vision restored (vv. 18–19)

III. We need to formulate a philosophy (Prov. 28:13)
    A. The options
        1. Sin concealed
        2. Sin confessed
    B. The consequences
        1. Concealed sin produces blight
        2. Confessed sin introduces light

Part 2

Selected Psalms

13

How to Be Happy though Human

Psalm 1

Happiness is one of the great quests of the human race. Yet for all the searching, it remains elusive to many people. Some have decided that it does not exist. Others have assumed it is not for them, but God has a formula for all. (Note: "blessed is . . . ," literally "happy.")

I. The happy man's philosophy
   A. He rejects a godless philosophy
      1. Philosophy without God is like a wheel without a hub
      2. Philosophy without God leaves a man short of the mark
      3. Philosophy without God makes a man cynical and hopeless
   B. He respects a godly philosophy (v. 2)
      1. Acknowledge the place of the Lord

    2. Accept the rule of the Lord
    3. Appreciate the leading of the Lord

II. The happy man's position
    A. He maintains a godly stance (v. 3)
        1. The stability of a deep-rooted tree
        2. The sufficiency of a deep-flowing river
        3. The productivity of a fruitful bough
        4. The reliability of an evergreen tree
    B. He recognizes the predicament of the godless (v. 4)
        1. They are without content when the wind comes
        2. They are without excuse when the judgment comes
        3. They are without hope when the kingdom comes

III. The happy man's peace
    A. He rejoices in the certainty of the faithfulness of God
    B. He rejoices in contrast to the lostness of the ungodly

15

Faith under Fire

Psalm 11

Many people in today's world feel that they are under fire and don't know where to take cover. Psalm 11 has some healthy suggestions.

   I. Attitudes of faith (v. 1)–"trust" in the Psalms has different shades of meaning
      A. "Take refuge in" (Ps. 11:1)–man's need of security
      B. "Lean upon" (Ps. 9:10)–man's need of support
      C. "Roll on" (Ps. 22:8)

  II. Attacks on faith (vv. 1b–3)
      A. Discouraging advice–"flee as a bird"
      B. Disturbing antagonism–"they bend the bow"
      C. Distressing anarchy–"foundations are destroyed"
      D. Disconcerting attitudes–"what can we do?"

   III. Adequacy through faith (vv. 4–7a)–N.B. Trust in an object releases the ability of that object: The LORD is the one whom David trusts (cf. Ps. 146:3; 20:7)

      A. The LORD as priest who intercedes–"in his temple"

      B. The LORD as king who reigns–"on his throne"

      C. The LORD as Father who cares–"His eyes behold"

      D. The LORD as judge who evaluates–"His eyelids try"

      E. The LORD as righteousness who saves–"the righteous Lord"

      F. The LORD as friend who loves–"the Lord loveth"

   IV. Anticipation by faith (v. 7b)–N.B. literally "the upright shall behold his countenance"

      A. The anticipation of being with him

      B. The anticipation of being like him (1 John 3:2)

16

The Heart of the Redeemed

Psalm 14

The man who experiences the love of God has born within him a love for the Lord, but his heart throbs with concern for people, too. In this psalm we get a glimpse of . . .

- I. A broken heart (vv. 1–5a)
  - A. Because of the foolishness of man (v. 1a)
  - B. Because of the fallenness of man (vv. 1b–3a)
  - C. Because of the filthiness of man (v. 3b)
  - D. Because of the forgetfulness of man (v. 4)
  - E. Because of the fearfulness of man (v. 5a)

- II. A full heart (vv. 5b–6)
  - A. Because man is God's residence
    1. To reveal himself to man
    2. To reach man for himself

    B. Because God is man's refuge
        1. From the results of his own foolishness
        2. From the heat of man's vindictiveness
        3. From the products of the world's
           hopelessness

III. A yearning heart (v. 7)
    A. That the Word of the Lord might be expounded
    B. That the liberty of the Lord might be
       experienced
    C. That the joy of the Lord might be expressed

17

The Secrets of Life

Psalm 16

Life has its problems and life has its secrets. In many lives the problems have outrun the secrets, so this *Miktam* (which probably means "secret") of David may help get things into perspective.

I. Cultivate the secret of the Lord's presence
   A. By reflecting on who he is—"my portion" (v. 5)
   B. By relating to what he offers—"I take refuge" (v. 1)
   C. By repenting of what he hates—"my goodness" (v. 2)
   D. By rejecting what he condemns—"I will not offer" (v. 4)
   E. By requesting what he promises—"Preserve me" (v. 1)
   F. By rejoicing in what he does—"makes saints" (v. 3)

II. Calculate the significance of the Lord's providence
   A. In terms of past experience
      1. He has counseled me (v. 7)
      2. He has controlled me (v. 8)
      3. He has comforted me (v. 6)
   B. In terms of present experience
      1. The support of his presence (v. 8b)
      2. The supply of his pleasures (v. 11)
   C. In terms of progressive experience
      1. Direction in the path of life (v. 11)
      2. Deliverance in the place of death (vv. 9–10)

III. Captivate the sense of the Lord's power
   A. Through a personal relationship
      (N.B. I, my, etc.)
   B. Through a powerful resurrection (v. 10; see Acts 2:25, 28)

19

The Agony and the Ecstasy

Psalm 22

Psalm 22 not only pictures the psalmist as a deer trapped by hunting dogs but also pictures Christ as the suffering and triumphant Savior.

    I. The agony of the rejected Savior (vv. 1–21)
       A. Deserted by his God (vv. 1–5)
          1. Unhelped (v. 1)
          2. Unheard (v. 2)
          3. Unholy (v. 3)
       B. Despised by his people (vv. 6–13)
          1. Yapping of the dogs (vv. 6–11)
          2. Goring of the bulls (v. 12)
          3. Devouring of the lion (v. 13)
       C. Destroyed by his cross (vv. 14–21)
          1. Dried up like a pot (v. 14)
          2. Ground up like dust (v. 15)
          3. Hung up like a criminal (vv. 16–17)

   II. The ecstasy of the risen Savior (vv. 22–24)
- A. The ecstasy of rising from the dead—"I *will* declare . . ." (v. 22a)
- B. The ecstasy of reuniting with the brethren (v. 22b)—"the midst of the congregation"
- C. The ecstasy of rejoicing in the Lord—"glorify him" (vv. 23–24)

  III. The victory of the righteous Savior (vv. 25–31)
- A. The personal experience of his victory (vv. 25–26)
  1. They that are meek shall be filled
  2. They that seek shall be thrilled
- B. The universal expansion of his victory (vv. 27–28)
  1. The kindreds of the nations become . . .
  2. The kingdom of the Lord
- C. The eternal extent of his victory (vv. 29–31)
  1. None can keep alive his soul . . .
  2. But your heart shall live forever

20

Good News for Modern Sheep

Psalm 23

God compares people with sheep. The analogy is hardly flattering but extremely accurate. This psalm shows what God does for sheep who are willing to admit to the description.

I. The sheep's expression of faith
    A. A practical expression (Shepherd)
        (see John 10:3-4)
    B. A profound expression—"Jehovah is Shepherd"
    C. A positive expression—"is"
    D. A personal expression—"my"

II. The sheep's experience of faith (vv. 2–5)
    A. The freshness of faith
        1. The freshness of green pastures (satisfaction)
        2. The freshness of still waters (peace)

      3. The freshness of anointed head (fragrance)
      4. The freshness of overflowing cup (joy)
  B. The fullness of faith
      1. The fullness of assurance—"I shall not want"
      2. The fullness of abundance—"a table"
      3. The fullness of awareness—"goodness and love will follow me"
  C. The fearlessness of faith
      1. Faith sees death as a shadow
      2. Faith sees enemies as defeated
      3. Faith sees the Lord as supreme

III. The sheep's expectations of faith (v. 6)
  A. The expectation of continual blessing
      1. The goodness of God
      2. The forgiveness of God
  B. The expectation of eternal blessedness
      1. The presence of God
      2. The provision of God

21
Whose World Is It?

Psalm 24

David was excited about returning the ark to Jerusalem, so he wrote this psalm. In it he touches on many important subjects.

    I. Whose world? (vv. 1–2)
       A. It was founded by God
          1. Creator (v. 2a)
          2. Controller (v. 2b)
          3. Claimant (v. 1)
             a. All earth resources (ecological)
             b. All earth regimes (political)
             c. All earth residences (sociological)
       B. It was entrusted to man (Gen. 1:26)
          1. He was made in God's image
          2. He was commissioned as God's agent
       C. It was traded to Satan (2 Cor. 4:4) and resulted in . . .
          1. Ecological disaster

      2. Political distrust

      3. Sociological disunity

II. Whose responsibility? (Ps. 24:3–6)
    A. His qualifications (v. 3)
      1. Ability to ascend the hill
      2. Ability to enter the holy place
    B. His qualities (v. 4)
      1. Utter purity
      2. Utter sincerity
      3. Utter humility
      4. Utter integrity
    C. His quest (v. 5)
      1. Blessing from the Lord
      2. Salvation for the people

III. Whose king? (vv. 7–10)
    A. Those who recognize his glory (vv. 7–8a)
    B. Those who respect his victory (vv. 8b–10)
    C. Those who receive him personally (v. 9)

22

The Voice of the Lord

Psalm 29

God loves to communicate with his people. He does it constantly, at different times and in different ways. And he expects to be heard.

I. The inflections of his voice
  A. The strong voice of conflict (v. 3)
  B. The small voice of conscience (1 Kings 19:12)
  C. The sweet voice of concern (Song of Sol. 2:14)
  D. The sharp voice of conviction (Rev. 1:10)

II. The impact of his voice
  A. A shaking impact (Ps. 29:8)—an earthquake in the wilderness
  B. A breaking impact (v. 5)—a hurricane in the forest
  C. A remaking impact (vv. 6–9)—a deluge on the mountains

III. The inspiration of his voice
   A. To beauty of worship (vv. 1–2)
      1. Through respect for his name
      2. Through reproduction of his nature
      3. Holiness=healthiness, wholeness
   B. To boldness of witness (vv. 9–11)–Note: "Everyone speaks" (v. 9)
      1. To God's glory (v. 10)
      2. To God's goodness (v. 11a)
      3. To God's grace (v. 11b)
      4. To God's greatness (v. 1)

23

The Joys of Forgiveness

Psalm 32

Only God can forgive sins. And only humans can experience forgiveness. The person who is forgiven and knows it experiences a special kind of joy.

I. The sinfulness that necessitates forgiveness (vv. 1–2)
  A. Transgression–doing what is forbidden
  B. Sin–not doing what is commanded
  C. Iniquity–perverting what is right
  D. Guile–projecting what is false

II. The forgiveness that leads to blessedness (vv. 1–2)
  A. Forgiven–carried away
  B. Covered–put out of sight
  C. Not imputed–not put to account

III. The blessedness that produces prayerfulness
     (vv. 3–5)
     A. Don't evade the issue (vv. 3–4)
     B. Do admit the sin (v. 5)
     C. Do ask for forgiveness (v. 5)
     D. Do believe you are forgiven (v. 5)

IV. The prayerfulness that includes faithfulness
     (vv. 6–7)
     A. To a forgiving God—"for this"
     B. To a reachable God—"may be found"
     C. To a powerful God—"my hiding place"

 V. The faithfulness that brings joyfulness (vv. 8–9)
     A. Faithful in involvement
     B. Faithful in instruction

VI. The joyfulness that comes from forgiveness
     (vv. 10–11)
     A. A joy experienced in righteousness
     B. A joy expressed in reality

24

Speaking Personally

Psalm 34

Autobiographical passages of Scripture are particularly helpful, as they show how God has worked in the lives of ordinary people and therefore may reasonably be expected to work in similar ways today. David speaks about . . .

I. Some personal experiences
   A. An experience of deliverance from fear (v. 4)
   B. An experience of salvation from trouble (v. 6)

II. Some passionate exhortations
   A. O magnify the Lord (v. 3)—an exhortation to reality of worship
   B. O taste and see (v. 8)—an exhortation to specific experimentation
   C. O fear the Lord (v. 9)—an exhortation to practical commitment

III. Some positive intentions
    A. I will bless the Lord (vv. 1–2)
        1. Continually
        2. Vocally
        3. Unashamedly
    B. I will teach the truth (vv. 11–23)
        1. Pupils
           a. Children who want to listen (v. 11)
           b. Adults who want to live (v. 12)
        2. Curriculum
           a. The personality of the Lord
               (1) His eyes (v. 15a)
               (2) His ears (v. 15b)
               (3) His face (v. 16)
           b. The power of the Lord
               (1) His saving power (v. 18)
               (2) His keeping power (v. 20)
               (3) His redeeming power (v. 22)

25

The Fountain of Life

Psalm 36

The psalmist spoke of God in many ways. To him he appeared in many forms meeting many needs. In this psalm he is the *fountain*, a very wonderful term to describe the totally indispensable nature of his being to man.

I. The fountain of life (v. 9)
   A. The initial source
      1. Of physical life (Gen. 1:26–28)
      2. Of spiritual life (John 1:34)
      3. Of eternal life (John 10:28)
   B. The continual resource–Note: "Continue" (Ps. 36:10); "preserve" (v. 6)–through . . .
      1. His mercifulness–vast as the heavens (v. 5a)
      2. His faithfulness–high as the clouds (v. 5b)
      3. His righteousness–solid as the mountains (v. 6a)

        4. His decisiveness–deep as the ocean (v. 6b)
        5. His lovingkindness–precious as jewels (v. 7)

  II. The fullness of life–a life of . . .
     A. Trusting under his wings (v. 7b)
     B. Feasting in his house (v. 8a)
     C. Drinking at his river (v. 8b)
     D. Walking in his light (v. 9b)
     E. Depending on his support (v. 11)

 III. The follies of life (see Jer. 2:13–14)
     A. Forsaking the only fountain
        1. Through neglecting it
        2. Through rejecting it
     B. Adopting unsatisfactory alternatives
        1. They don't hold water
        2. They do produce drought (see Ps. 36:1–4)

26

Don't Get Upset

Psalm 37

Experience talks. David wrote this psalm when he was an old man (v. 25) and gave some commonsense instructions concerning living in frustrating circumstances.

I. Why the godly get upset
   A. Because the ungodly seem to have it so good
      1. Their actions produce envy (v. 1)
      2. Their advancement produces questions (v. 7)
      3. Their authority produces frustration (v. 35)
   B. Because the godly have it so tough: They are called to a life of . . .
      1. Conflict (v. 14)
      2. Sacrifice (v. 21)
      3. Discipline (v. 31)

II. What the godly must understand
   A. God will ultimately triumph (vv. 18–20)

B. Good will eventually prevail (vv. 9–15)
C. Godly will eternally survive (vv. 23–24)
D. Godliness will inevitably satisfy (vv. 37–40)
E. Grace will continually flow (vv. 23–25)

III. What the godly must undertake
   A. In terms of attitude
      1. Trust and do (v. 3)
      2. Delight and desire (v. 4)
      3. Commit and trust (v. 5)
      4. Rest and wait (v. 7)
   B. In terms of action
      1. Don't get hot (v. 1)
      2. Don't get mad (v. 8)
      3. Don't get misled (v. 27)
   C. In terms of approach
      1. Grace (v. 21)
      2. Goodness (vv. 3, 27)

27

How Are You Feeling?

Psalm 40

This question can be either a casual greeting or a serious inquiry. Both in the physical and spiritual world it can help diagnose health or illness.

   I. That sinking feeling (vv. 1–2a)
      A. Nothing to do but struggle
      B. No one to call but God

  II. That singing feeling (vv. 2b–3a)
      A. Singing because God listened to me
      B. Singing because God lifted me
      C. Singing because God liberated me

 III. That sharing feeling (vv. 3b–5)
      A. The sharing that people see (v. 3b)
      B. The sharing that people hear (vv. 5, 9–10)
      C. The sharing that people respect (v. 4)

IV. That submissive feeling (vv. 6–8)
    A. Through ears that discern God's will
    B. Through hearts that desire God's will
    C. Through wills that do God's will

V. That shaky feeling (vv. 11–15)
    A. Shaky because of sins that master me
    B. Shaky because of scoffers that mock me

VI. That saved feeling (v. 16)
    A. Saved to live
    B. Saved to laugh
    C. Saved to love

VII. That secure feeling (v. 17)
    A. Secure in God's compassion
    B. Secure in God's competence
    C. Secure in God's coming

28

Communicating Christ

Psalm 45

This psalm speaks of the marriage of Christ and his church. It is a glad expression of praise and a beautiful piece of communication.

   I. The manner of communicating (v. 1)
      A. The exuberance of the heart
      B. The excellence of the material
      C. The experience of the speaker
      D. The expertise of the communication

  II. The material being communicated
      A. The majesty of Christ (vv. 2–9)
         1. Christ the Man
           a. The graciousness of his lips
           b. The greatness of his life
         2. Christ the King (vv. 3–5)
           a. The majestic power of his sword (v. 3)

        b. The majestic progress of his truth (v. 4)

        c. The majestic promise of his triumph (v. 5)

    3. Christ the Lord (vv. 6–7)

        a. Lord of the eternal throne

        b. Lord of the righteous scepter

        c. Lord of the anointed head

    4. Christ the Bridegroom (vv. 8–9)

        a. Leaving his palace

        b. Looking for his bride

B. The miracle of the church (vv. 10–17)

    1. A responsive church (v. 10)

    2. A resplendent church (v. 12)

    3. A respected church (v. 12)

    4. A rich church (v. 13)

    5. A rejoicing church (vv. 14–15)

    6. A reproductive church (vv. 16–17)

29

When Trouble Comes

Psalm 46

When trouble comes "with the finality of an earthquake" (v. 2), "with the fury of a storm" (v. 3a), and "with the force of a flood" (v. 3b), how do we cope?

I. You must realize
   A. That God is a refuge for his people (v. 1)
      1. Continually available (see Heb. 6:18)
      2. Thoroughly adequate—"our strength"
      3. Readily accessible—"very present"
   B. That God is resident among his people (Ps. 46:5)
      1. The God of purpose—"most high" (v. 4)
      2. The God of power—"Lord of hosts" (v. 7)
      3. The God of patience—"God of Jacob" (v. 7)
   C. That God sends a river to his people (v. 4)
      1. A refreshing river—"makes glad"

2. A reviving river (see Ezek. 47:9;
   John 7:37–39)

II. You must respond
    A. Reflect on what this means
       1. God is a refuge, therefore . . . fear is illogi-
          cal (v. 2)
       2. God is a resident, therefore . . . city is im-
          movable (v. 5)
       3. God has a river, therefore . . . Christianity is
          invincible (v. 5b)
    B. Review what God has done (vv. 8–9)
    C. Rejoice in what he promises (v. 10b)

III. You must relax–"be still" is literally "relax"
     A. Resist the natural impulses–"Be still" (v. 10a)
     B. Restore the spiritual relationship–"and know"
        (v. 10b)

30

Celebration

Psalm 47

Celebration is the commemoration of a joyous event: In religious terminology it means the performance of a ritualistic ceremony. This psalm combines the two meanings and shows worship to be a joyous ceremony in praise of God.

I. Celebration must be rooted in intelligence–Note: "Sing with understanding" (v. 7)
   A. Understanding the terror of the Lord (v. 2)
   B. Understanding the teachings of the Lord (v. 3)– Note: "under our feet" (see Acts 22:3)
   C. Understanding the trustworthiness of the Lord (v. 4a)
   D. Understanding the tenderness of the Lord (v. 4b)
   E. Understanding the triumph of the Lord (v. 5)

II. Celebration must be related to experience
   A. Experience of the supremacy of the Lord (v. 8)

13

    B. Experience of the submission of the will (v. 9)
    C. Experience of the surrender of the life (v. 4)

III. Celebration must be recognizable by response
    A. A united response–Note: "All ye people"
    B. An uninhibited response
        1. Clapping–an uninhibited excitement
        2. Shouting–an uninhibited exhibition
        3. Shouting–an uninhibited exclamation
        4. Singing–an uninhibited expression
    C. An unending response (see Rev. 5:9–14)

31

The Church Is Beautiful

Psalm 48

Jerusalem, the ancient city of Zion, has been the center of man's attention for thousands of years. In addition to her great historical, archaeological, and political importance, she has great spiritual significance as a "type" of the church.

I. The place of delight (vv. 1–2)
   A. The place of God's presence
   B. The place of God's praise
   C. The place of God's preeminence
   D. The place of God's purposes

II. The place of defense (vv. 3–7)
   A. The place where God's strength is known
   B. The place where God's superiority is shown
      1. By controlling her enemies
      2. By confounding her critics

III. The place of discovery (v. 8)
   A. The place where theory becomes reality
   B. The place where theology breeds certainty

IV. The place of deliberation (vv. 9–11)
   A. Deliberation on God's lovingkindness
   B. Deliberation on God's faithfulness
   C. Deliberation on God's righteousness
   D. Deliberation on God's carefulness

 V. The place of declaration (vv. 12–13)
   A. Know what to tell
       1. From personal experience
       2. From painstaking examination
   B. Tell what you know

VI. The place of decision (v. 14)
   A. This God . . . our God
   B. This Guide . . . our Guide

32

All Humans Are Equal

Psalm 49

Despite obvious social, economic, and intellectual inequalities, humans are fundamentally equal. Concentration on the areas of equality is necessary for spiritual development.

    I. All humans are equal before God (vv. 1–5)
        A. As residents of God's world (vv. 1–2)–low, high, rich, and poor are together
        B. As recipients of God's Word (vv. 3–4)–wisdom, understanding, parables, and dark sayings are for all
        C. As resisters of God's will (v. 5)–iniquity catches up with everyone eventually

   II. All humans are equal in the grave (vv. 6–20)
        A. The frailty of humans (vv. 6–11)
            1. Their wealth cannot rescue them

   2. Their wisdom cannot resurrect them
   3. Their worldliness cannot reinforce them
    (v. 20)
  B. The futility of life (vv. 12–13)
   1. The futility of misplaced trust
   2. The futility of mistaken ideas
   3. The futility of misleading praise
  C. The finality of death (v. 14)
   1. The final domination
   2. The final destruction
   3. The final disintegration
   4. The final disappointment (vv. 17–19)

III. All humans are equal in the glory (v. 15)
  A. The only humans in the glory will have been . . .
   1. Redeemed by the Lord
   2. Received by the Lord
  B. But there the equality ends, for some will be in the glory, but others will be in "Sheol"

33

Checkup Time

Psalm 50

Regular physical checkups are advisable. Financial checkups are normal. Spiritual checkups are imperative, particularly in the light of the judgment of God. It is checkup time again.

   I. God's checkup of the faithful (vv. 1–15) Note: El Elohim Jehovah (v. 1)
     A. God has spoken (vv. 1–4)
       1. He spoke of his power through the creation (v. 1)
       2. He spoke of his promises through covenants (v. 5b)
       3. He spoke of his purposes through the church (v. 2)
       4. He spoke of his purity through the Christ (v. 3)
     B. God has sanctified (v. 5)
       1. Those committed to be saints
       2. Those covenanted through sacrifice

    C. God has summoned (vv. 6–15)
       1. In order that he might rebuke
         a. Misguided formalism (vv. 8–9)
         b. Mistaken materialism (vv. 10–13)
       2. In order that he might remind
         a. The sacrifice of thanksgiving (v. 14a)
         b. The sacrifice of faithfulness (v. 14b)
         c. The sacrifice of praise (v. 23a)
       3. In order that he might revive
         a. Call and I will deliver (v. 15a)
         b. I will be glorified (v. 15b)

  II. God's checkup of the forgetful (vv. 16–23)
    A. They are unreal (v. 16)
    B. They are unwilling (v. 17)
    C. They are unrepentant (vv. 18–21)
    D. They are unregenerate (vv. 22–23)

34

The Blessedness of Brokenness

Psalm 51

While man delights to boost his ego, God desires a broken spirit because he knows that only through submissiveness can his purposes be worked out.

I. The blessedness of a broken spirit (v. 17)—
   brokenness is . . .
   A. A response to an understanding of God
      1. His mercy (v. 1)
      2. His justice (v. 4)
      3. His demands (v. 6)
      4. His power (v. 8)
   B. A result of the uncovering of self
      1. Unworthiness (v. 1)
      2. Uncleanness (v. 2)
      3. Unfaithfulness (v. 3)
      4. Unrighteousness (v. 4)

    C. A rejection of an untenable position
       1. Sinfulness must be condemned—no longer condoned
       2. Selfishness must be repudiated—no longer cultivated
       3. Submissiveness must be realistic—no longer ritualistic

  II. The restoration of a right spirit (v. 10)
    A. Sinfulness is no longer attractive
    B. Selfishness is no longer compulsive
    C. Submissiveness is no longer restrictive

 III. The healthiness of the Holy Spirit (v. 11)
    —see Saul's experience of the Holy Spirit
    (1 Sam. 16:1, 14; 2 Sam. 7:15)
    A. A healthy sense of the divine presence
    B. A healthy sense of the divine power
    C. A healthy sense of the divine pleasure

 IV. The life of the liberating spirit (v. 12)
    A. Freedom from self-centeredness (v. 12a)
    B. Freedom from self-trust (v. 12b)
    C. Freedom from self-interest (v. 13)
    D. Freedom from self-pity (v. 14)
    E. Freedom from self-consciousness (v. 15)

35

The Devotional Life

Psalm 63

David was on the run in the wilderness. Danger and frustration lurked on every hand. But still he persevered with the chief priority, his relationship with his God. This he did through his devotional life. So must we.

I. The definition of a devotional life—it involves . . .
   A. The seeking of a soul (v. 1a)
      1. Seeking produces original contact with God (Isa. 55:6)
      2. Seeking produces continual experience of God (2 Chron. 26:5)
   B. The satisfying of a soul (Ps. 63:5)
      1. Because of restored equilibrium
      2. Because of revitalized experience
      3. Because of renewed perspective
   C. The strengthening of a soul (v. 8b)
      1. Reminder of my position—"right hand"
      2. Reminder of his power—"upholds me"

II. The desire for a devotional life
   A. Comes from personal relationship (v. 1a)
   B. Comes from personal need (v. 1b)
   C. Comes from personal experience (v. 2b)
   D. Comes from personal devotion (v. 3)
   E. Comes from personal obedience (Ps. 27:8)

III. The discipline of a devotional life
   A. The discipline of determination (Ps. 63:8)
      1. My lips will glorify you (v. 3)
      2. I will praise you (v. 4a)
      3. I will lift up my hands (v. 4b)
      4. My soul will be satisfied (v. 5a)
      5. My mouth will praise you (v. 5b)
   B. The discipline of time
      1. Personally in the morning (v. 1)
      2. Publicly in the daytime (v. 2)
      3. Privately in the nighttime (v. 6)
   C. The discipline of mind
      1. A mind that seeks truth
      2. A mind that remembers the truth
      3. A mind that meditates on the truth

36

Praise the Lord

Psalm 66

C. S. Lewis wrote, "Praise is the appointed consummation of our enjoyment of God." Therefore, it should be a regular and meaningful part of the believer's life! "Praise the Lord," or "Hallelujah," is a scriptural command, not a noisy, unwelcome instruction or a fatuous remark.

I. Praise the Lord in your worship
   A. Why should I praise him?
      1. Because praise glorifies God (Ps. 50:23)
      2. Because praise demonstrates salvation (Isa. 61:1–3)
      3. Because praise encourages others (Col. 3:16)
      4. Because praise enriches worshipers (Ps. 147:1)
   B. How should I praise him?
      1. By meditating

    2. By articulating—shout (Ps. 66:1); sing (v. 2); say (v. 3)
       a. Your adoration of his person (name) (v. 2)
       b. Your awareness of his power (vv. 3–4)
       c. Your appreciation of his purposes (vv. 5–7)
  C. Where should I praise him? (see Ps. 150:1; Acts 16:25)

 II. Praise the Lord in your walk
  A. The regenerated life (v. 9a)
    1. The deadness of the unregenerate soul (James 5:20)
    2. The aliveness of the regenerate soul
  B. The reassured life (v. 9b)
    1. Life with a sense of security
    2. Life with a firm foundation (Jude 24)
  C. The refined life (Ps. 66:10–12)
    1. The testing that God ordains (vv. 10–12a)
    2. The triumph that God offers (v. 12b)

III. Praise the Lord in your witness
  A. The witness of sacrifice (vv. 13–15)
  B. The witness of speech (vv. 16–20)
    1. The progress he has made in you (v. 16)
    2. The prayers he has answered for you (v. 19)
    3. The principles he explained to you (v. 18)

37

What the World Needs

Psalm 67

What the world needs is love, peace, equality, law and order, food—according to various voices. They're probably right. But more than these things the world needs a spiritual revival. How does this happen?

    I. The proclamation of God's way (v. 2a)
        A. This way confirms God's wisdom
            1. Because it is a high way (cf. Isa. 55:7–9; Prov. 14:12)
            2. Because it is a holy way (cf. Isa. 35:8–9; Isa. 53:6)
        B. This way constricts man's waywardness
            1. A broad way to destruction (Matt. 7:13)
            2. A narrow way to life (Matt. 7:14)
            3. The only way to God (John 14:6)
        C. This way controls man's will
            1. By making him a disciple (Acts 9:2)
            2. By giving him direction

II. The participation in God's work (v. 2b)
   A. The delivering aspect of salvation
   B. The healing aspect of salvation

III. The propagation of God's worship (v. 3)
   A. The author of salvation
   B. The dispenser of truth
   C. The ground of justice
   D. The lord of harvest

IV. The preparation of God's workers (v. 1)
   A. Workers asking for divine mercy
   B. Workers anxious for divine blessing
   C. Workers eager for divine approval

38

The Lord in Perspective

Psalm 68

P erspective gives balance and depth. Absence of per-spective produces distortion and error. The Lord must be seen in perspective–in all his transcendent glory but also in his humble descent into the affairs of man cul-minating in his triumphant ascent into glory.

I. The Lord transcending
   A. He transcends the universe–"he rideth upon the heavens" (v. 4)
   B. He transcends the mind–"his name is Jehovah" (v. 4): See also Exodus 6:3
   C. He transcends the grave–"from the Sovereign LORD comes escape from death" (v. 20)

II. The Lord descending
   A. To establish his people
      1. Whom he could love (vv. 5–6)
      2. Whom he could load (vv. 7–8)
      3. Where he could live (v. 16)

    B. To deliver his word
        1. The revelation of his mind
        2. The communication of his truth
    C. To provide his salvation
        1. The humility of his son (Phil. 2:5–8)
        2. The grace of his action (Ps. 68:19)

III. The Lord ascending (see also Eph. 4:7–13)
    A. The glory of the ascended Lord
        1. His glorious victory
        2. His glorious vitality
        3. His glorious vindication
    B. The greatness of the ascended Lord
        1. Releasing captives to himself
        2. Recycling captives for himself
    C. The gifts of the ascended Lord
        1. For the general blessing of man
        2. For the specific building of the church

39

Thy Kingdom Come

Psalm 72

Solomon, David's son, reigned in his father's stead with great distinction. His feats as an administrator, author, and architect are legendary. This psalm is a prayer for him, but also for a king "greater than Solomon," whose reign shall surpass all other reigns (Luke 11:31).

I. The basis of his reign is spiritual (vv. 1–7)–righteousness, the key note (vv. 1–3)
   A. The righteousness he portrays
   B. The righteousness he procures (Rom. 3:19–26)
   C. The righteousness he provides (Rom. 5:17)
   D. The righteousness he produces (Matt. 6:1)

II. The boundaries of his reign are universal (Ps. 72:8–11)
   A. Transcending all geographical boundaries (v. 8)

B. Transcending all spiritual boundaries (v. 9)
C. Transcending all political boundaries
   (vv. 10–11)

III. The blessings of his reign are eternal (vv. 12–17)
   A. Material blessings
      1. Restoring a sense of compassion (vv. 12–13)
      2. Redressing the powers of violence (v. 14)
      3. Replenishing the earth (v. 16)
   B. Spiritual blessings
      1. Renewal of prayer through him (v. 15a)
      2. Revival of praise to him (v. 15b)

IV. The builders of his kingdom
   A. Those who profess the kingdom
   B. Those who pray for the kingdom
   C. Those who preach the kingdom
   D. Those who practice the kingdom

Part 3

Sound Sense
for Successful Living

41

The Place of Knowledge

A proverb (Hebrew *māšāl*) was a familiar Hebrew liter-
ary device designed to "arrest attention, awaken responsive thought, and remain fixed in memory."
Solomon, regarded as the wisest of men (see 1 Kings
3:3–13; 4:32), was a master of the proverb. Along with
other wise sayings, his proverbs provide practical instruction concerning godly living. He insisted that knowledge is the key.

I. The place of knowledge
   A. Relating to human deficiencies
      1. The gullibility of the simple (v. 4)
      2. The impetuosity of the young (v. 4)
      3. The inadequacy of the wise (v. 5)
      4. The inconsistency of the man of under-
         standing (v. 5)
      5. The obduracy of the fool (v. 7)
   B. Relating to divine intentions

    1. To display knowledge (Isa. 11:1–5)
    2. To dispense knowledge (Prov. 2:5–6)

 II. The products of knowledge
    A. Discipline–"instruction" (e.g., 3:11; 23:13; Isa. 53:5)
    B. Discrimination–"understanding" (e.g., 1 Kings 3:9)
    C. Discernment–"wisdom" (e.g., 1 Sam. 25:3 ff.)
    D. Discretion–"subtlety," "discernment" (Gen. 3:1; Prov. 12:2)
    E. Discovery–"knowledge," "learning" (e.g., Prov. 2:5; 3:6)

III. The procurement of knowledge
    A. The recognition of its basis (v. 7)
       1. Respect for Jehovah as the key to knowledge
       2. Reverence for Jehovah as the King of life
    B. The response to its requirements
       1. Perceiving (v. 2)
       2. Receiving (v. 3)
       3. Hearing (v. 5)
       4. Attaining (v. 5)
       5. Understanding (v. 6)
       6. Despising (v. 7)

Note: Plato said, "Let no one who is not a geometrician enter." Solomon said, "You who are simple, gain prudence; you who are foolish, gain understanding" (Prov. 8:5).

42

Life Forces

Proverbs 1:8-33

The philosophical term *life force,* or *élan vital,* has specialized meaning, but the Bible teaches much about many other forces that need to be reckoned with in daily living.

I. The force of formative influences
   A. The variety of formative influences (Note: "Father," and "son" are used in a variety of ways)
      1. Parental influences (v. 8)
         a. Directive nature of parental influence
         b. Positive nature of parental influence (v. 9)
      2. Historical influences
         a. Founding fathers
         b. Church fathers
      3. Spiritual influences (e.g., Paul and Philemon)
         a. Determined by quality of influence
         b. Determined by response to influence

II. The force of evil enticements
   A. The nature of evil enticements
      1. Attractive (v. 10)
         a. Acceptance
         b. Excitement
         c. Easy gain
      2. Cumulative (vv. 11–14)
      3. Compulsive (vv. 17–19)
         a. Irrationality (v. 17)
         b. Insatiability (v. 19a)
      4. Destructive (v. 19b)
   B. The reaction to evil enticements
      1. Do not give in (v. 1)
      2. Do not set foot (v. 15)

III. The force of divine proclamation
   A. The uncomplicated nature of divine proclamation
      1. The fact of evil
      2. The fear of the Lord
   B. The uncomplimentary nature of divine proclamation
      1. The simple love simplicity
      2. The fools hate knowledge
      3. The scorners delight in scorn
   C. The uncompromising nature of divine proclamation
      1. Uncompromising prerequisite–turn at my reproof (v. 23a)
      2. Uncompromising promises
         a. The outpoured spirit (v. 23)
         b. The unveiled word (v. 23)
         c. The immovable security (v. 33)
      3. Uncompromising predictions
         a. Despair for the unrepentant (vv. 24–31)
         b. Destruction for the self-sufficient (v. 32)

43

The Paths of Life

Proverbs 2:1-22

Innumerable options present themselves to people living in today's world. But according to Scripture these options represent two main possibilities for life: One is the possibility of living God's way, and the other is the possibility of going your own way. Solomon clearly delineated the difference.

I. The necessity of recognizing the different paths—this involves:
   A. Recognizing biblical wisdom
      1. Reality of good and evil
      2. Reality of God and Satan
      3. Reality of heaven and hell
      4. Reality of life and death
   B. Rejecting popular wisdom
      1. Everything is relative
      2. God is irrelevant; Satan is nonexistent

    3. Heaven—a state of mind; hell—a medieval concept

    4. Life is what you make it; death—try to ignore it

II. The certainty of discovering the right path
  A. God is committed to revealing the right path
    1. The basis of discovering truth is revelation (v. 6)
    2. The means of discovering truth is exploration (vv. 1–4)
      a. Willingness to receive the Word (v. 1)
      b. Readiness to apply the heart (v. 2)
      c. Carefulness to beseech the Lord (v. 3)
      d. Eagerness to pursue the clues (v. 4)
    3. The reality of discovering truth is consecration (v. 5)
  B. God is committed to leading in the right path—he is:
    1. A storehouse (v. 7a)
    2. A shield (v. 7b)
    3. A sentinel (v. 8)
  C. Man must be committed to following the right path
    1. The decision that is mandatory (v. 10a)
    2. The delight that is necessary (v. 10b)

III. The possibility of taking the wrong path
  A. By following the leading of the godless
    1. The godless man
      a. Who rejects uprightness (v. 13)
      b. Who rejoices in unrighteousness (v. 14)
    2. The godless woman
      a. Who flatters with words (v. 16)
      b. Who forsakes "the friend of her youth" (v. 17a)

       c. Who forgets the "covenant of her God"
         (v. 17b)

   B. By forgetting the consequences of godlessness
     1. Loss in this life (v. 19)
     2. Lostness in the life to come (v. 22)

44

Healthy, Wealthy, and Wise

Proverbs 3:1-35

According to the popular proverb, disciplined sleeping habits guarantee all-round well-being. Solomon had a better idea. He said that "knowing God" (v. 6) was the key to being "healthy, wealthy, and wise."

    I. How to be healthy
        A. The diverse ingredients
            1. A healthy body (v. 8)
            2. A healthy mind (vv. 2, 17, 23–25)
            3. A healthy spirit (vv. 18–22)
        B. The direct instructions
            1. Obey the Lord (vv. 1–4)
            2. Trust the Lord (v. 5)
            3. Know the Lord (v. 6)
            4. Fear the Lord (v. 7)
        C. The divine involvement
            1. The divine direction (v. 6)
            2. The divine protection (v. 26)

  II. How to be wealthy
      A. Be committed to scriptural principles
         1. Honor the Lord (v. 9)
         2. Share the blessing (vv. 27–28)
      B. Be convinced of scriptural promises (v. 10)
         1. Because God's principles are sound
         2. Because God's promises are sure
      C. Be clear about scriptural perspectives
         1. "Piety produces plenty" is generally true
         2. Riches require regulation (vv. 11–12)
         3. Wealth without wisdom is worthless
            (vv. 13–16)

  III. How to be wise
      A. Recognize wisdom in divine creation
         (vv. 19–20)
      B. Reject wisdom in our "own eyes" (v. 7)
      C. Receive wisdom as God's gift (v. 13)
      D. Reflect wisdom in personal relationships
         (vv. 29–31)
      E. Retain wisdom in life's alternatives (vv. 32–35)

45

Bright Prospects

Proverbs 4:1-27

Modern man is understandably concerned about the future. For many the prospects are gloomy in the extreme. But according to Scripture, "the path of the just" gets brighter along the way, until the final glorious day (v. 18).

    I. Prospects are the products of the past (v. 1–9) (e.g., the world of architecture, agriculture, athletics)
        A. Openness to be taught (vv. 1–3)
            1. What has been proven in experience—"a father"
            2. What is known to be "good doctrine"
        B. Willingness to be obedient (vv. 4–5)
            1. Retain
            2. Keep
            3. Forget not
            4. Neither decline
        C. Eagerness to be principled (vv. 6–9)

    1. "Get wisdom" a priority (e.g., Matt. 6:33)
    2. "Get wisdom" a necessity
       (e.g., Matt. 13:45–46)

II. Prospects are the projections of the present
    (Prov. 4:10–27)
    A. Continual appreciation of truth (vv. 10–13)
    B. Constant avoidance of evil (vv. 14–19)
       1. Recognize the existence of evil men
          a. Their intention is to destroy (v. 16)
          b. Their tools are wickedness and violence
             (v. 17)
          c. Their end is deep darkness (v. 19)
       2. Refuse involvement with evil men
          a. Enter not
          b. Avoid
          c. Pass not by
          d. Turn from
          e. Pass away (vv. 14–15)
    C. Consistent application of principles (vv. 20–27)
       1. The principle of the inclined ear (v. 20)
       2. The principle of the well-kept heart (v. 23)
          a. The seat of the spiritual being
          b. The source of spiritual behavior
             (e.g., John 7:38)
       3. The principle of the cleaned-up mouth
          (Prov. 4:24)
       4. The principle of the clearly focused eye
          (v. 25)
       5. The principle of the carefully pondered feet
          (v. 26)

III. Prospects are the provokers of the present
    A. Provoking to holiness of life (1 John 3:2–3)
    B. Provoking to depth of fellowship
       (1 Thess. 4:16–18)
    C. Provoking to intensity of service
       (Luke 12:37–40)

46

Straight Talk about Sex

Proverbs 5:1-23

It has been said that all societies have faced the problem of reconciling the need of controlling sex with that of giving it adequate expression. But it must be admitted that all societies have not achieved the right balance. The Scriptures, rightly understood, do.

I. The scriptural exposition of sex as sin
   A. "Sweet-talking sex" as sin (5:3-6)
      1. The enticing delusion (v. 3)
         a. Freedom from restriction
         b. Fulfillment of expression
      2. The hidden dangers
         a. Ultimate disillusion (v. 4)
         b. Spiritual deadness (v. 5)
         c. Personal dilemma (v. 6)
         d. Moral disintegration (vv. 9-14)
      3. The prescribed defense
         a. Bow thine ear (v. 1)

      b. Keep thy lips (v. 2)

      c. Remove thy way (v. 8)

  B. "Sophisticated sex" as sin (Prov. 6:20–35)

    1. The excitement of adultery

      a. The possession of the beautiful (v. 25a)

      b. The fun of the game (v. 25b)

      c. The thrill of the hunt (v. 26)

    2. The experience of the adulterer

      a. From "precious life" to "piece of bread" (v. 26)

      b. From "hot shot" to "hot coals" (vv. 27–29)

      c. From "self-satisfaction" to "self-destruction" (vv. 30–35)

    3. The explanation to adults (vv. 20–25)

      a. Going, sleeping, waking (vv. 20–22)

      b. Lamp, light, life (v. 23)

      c. Lust not, let not (v. 25)

  C. "Seductive sex" as sin (see Prov. 7)

II. The scriptural exposition of sex as love (Prov. 5:15–23)

  A. The foundation of mutual commitment–Note: "Thine own"

    1. Love means mutual commitment

    2. Sex means mutual abandonment

    3. Abandonment without commitment means disenchantment

  B. The freedom of mutual enjoyment

    1. Drink deeply (v. 15)

    2. Rejoice greatly (v. 18)

    3. Be captivated thoroughly (v. 19)

  C. The fruit of mutual fulfillment (v. 16)

47

Straight Talk about Sex 2

Proverbs 5:15-23

Sex uncontrolled will lead to all manner of illegitimate sexual activity outside of marriage, but sex unappreciated will lead to inadequate sexual expression within the confines of marriage. Sex within marriage involves:

    I. The foundation of mutual commitment
        A. The nature of mutual commitment
            1. The exhaustive nature—"thine own" (Song of Sol. 2:16)
            2. The exclusive nature—"only thine own"
            3. The expensive nature—"well, cistern" (Prov. 19:14)
            4. The extensive nature—"wife of thy youth" (Prov. 2:17)
        B. The nurture of mutual commitment
            1. The well-being of the well (Gen. 26:15–18)
            2. The care of the cistern (Jer. 2:13)
            3. The forsaking of the fountain (Jer. 2:13)

C. The necessity of mutual commitment
   1. Love means mutual commitment (John 3:16)
   2. Sex means mutual abandonment
   3. Abandonment without commitment spells disenchantment
      a. "Knowing" without knowing
      b. "Making love" without loving
      c. "Intercourse" without intercourse
      d. "Intimacy" without being intimate

II. The freedom of mutual enjoyment
  A. The enjoyment of unity (Gen. 2:24)
  B. The enjoyment of creativity
    1. Fountains dispersed
    2. Rivers in the streets
  C. The enjoyment of ecstasy
    1. Drink deeply (Prov. 5:15)
    2. Rejoice greatly (v. 18; Deut. 24:5)
    3. Be captivated thoroughly (Prov. 5:19)
    4. Be blessed spiritually (v. 18)

III. The fruit of mutual fulfillment
  A. Protection from destructive forces
    1. The force of contradictory behavior (v. 20)
    2. The force of ill-considered habit (v. 21)
    3. The force of constrictive activities (v. 22)
    4. The force of conclusive results (v. 23)
  B. Projection of constructive factors
    1. The factor of a full life
    2. The factor of a faithful marriage
    3. The factor of a fulfilled family

48

Assorted Disasters and How to Avoid Them

Proverbs 6:1–19

Giving warning of impending disaster is one of the most necessary and least appreciated functions of human society. The Scriptures do not sidestep the issue but meet it head on. So must we.

I. Beware of ill-considered kindness (vv. 1–5)
   A. Kindness—a Christian grace, evidence of:
      1. Goodness (Ps. 112:5)
      2. Affection (Rom. 12:10)
   B. Kindness—a potential snare
      1. For the benefactor
      2. For the beneficiary
   C. Kindness—a tough predicament
      1. Deliver yourself
      2. Deny your friend

II. Be wise to ill-fated laziness (Prov. 6:6–11)
   A. Laziness–its condition
     1. Insidious
     2. Dangerous
   B. Laziness–its contradiction
     1. Of God
     2. Of nature (vv. 6–8)
     3. Of spirituality (Rom. 12:11)
   C. Laziness–its consequences
     1. Unpreparedness (v. 11)
     2. Inadequacy

III. Be warned of ill-mannered wickedness
    (vv. 12–19)–Note: "naughty" related to "naught"
   A. Wickedness–its chronic power
     1. Conceived in the heart
     2. Conveyed by the body
     3. Condemned by the Lord
   B. Wickedness–its basic nature
     1. That which the Lord hates because:
       a. It contradicts his person
       b. It frustrates his purposes
     2. That which the Lord judges because he is holy and just
     3. That which the Lord forgives in Christ because he is gracious and merciful
   C. Wickedness–its intrinsic badness
     1. Pride–that which denies Deity
     2. Lies–that which denies truth
     3. Murder–that which denies the image of God
     4. Deceitfulness–that which denies a person's worth
     5. Evil enthusiasm–that which denies goodness
     6. Perjury–that which denies authority
     7. Troublemaking–that which denies love

49

Personal Responsibility

Proverbs 8–9

Passing the buck has been popular since Adam blamed Eve and Eve blamed the serpent. Today we blame the government, the weather, our genes, or the school board for most things. But in the main things, God points to each of us and informs us, "The buck stops here" (see 8:36; 9:12).

I. The responsibility of exercising personal discernment
   A. The availability of truth (8:1–5)
      1. Truth is attractive (8:6–12)
         a. Noble (8:6)
         b. Right (8:6)
         c. Straight (8:9)
         d. Rich (8:10–11)
         e. Prudent (8:12)
         f. Discreet (8:12)
      2. Truth is abrasive

a. Wickedness is abomination (8:7)
b. Evil is hated (8:13)
3. Truth is authoritative
a. Sound
b. Strong (8:14)
c. Just (8:15–16)
d. Leading (8:20)
e. Causing (8:21)
f. Eternal (8:22–31)
B. The accessibility of error (9:13–18)
1. Persuasive (9:13–16)
2. Seductive (9:17)
3. Destructive (9:18)
C. The activity of mankind
1. Positive activity
a. Hear (8:33)
b. Watch (8:34)
c. Wait (8:34)
d. Find (8:35)
e. Keep (8:32)
2. Negative activity
a. Miss (8:36)
b. Hate (8:36)
c. Scorn (9:12)

II. The responsibility of executing personal decision
A. Accept the invitation to "come" (9:5)
1. To that which is prepared (9:1–2)
2. To that which is proclaimed (9:3–5)
B. Obey the instruction to "forsake" (9:6a)
C. Follow the injunction to "go" (9:6b)
1. In the fear of the Lord (9:10a)
2. In the knowledge of the holy (9:10b)

III. The responsibility of experiencing personal destiny–Note: John 3:16; 5:24; 1 John 5:11–13

A. The personal aspects of destiny
   1. Whoever finds me finds life (Prov. 8:35)
   2. Whoever misses me wrongs his own soul
   3. Wise for thyself (9:12)
   4. Thou alone shalt bear (9:12)
B. The eternal aspects of destiny
   1. Life that is eternal
   2. Death that means "perishing"

50

Rich Man, Poor Man

Proverbs 10-11

Schemes for making money abound. Opportunities for amazing wealth are part of our society. But some rich men are poor rich men and some poor men are rich poor men. What does it mean to be rich?

I. The making of a rich man, poor man (N.B. The terms "rich" and "poor" are relative)
  A. The divine element—the blessings of the Lord (10:2)
    1. The granting of capability
    2. The presenting of opportunity (Deut. 8:18)
  B. The social element—the shame of the sleeper (Prov. 10:5)
    1. The evidence of teachability (10:1)
    2. The demonstration of sensitivity (10:5)
  C. The personal element—the hand of the diligent (10:4)
    1. The accepting of responsibility
    2. The engaging in productivity

II. The making of a poor rich man
   A. The potential for confusion (10:15)
      1. Inadequacies of riches
      2. Inaccuracies of riches (10:2; 11:4, 28)
   B. The problems of conservation (11:16)
      1. Retention requires attention
      2. Retention produces contention (11:26)
   C. The possibilities for corruption (28:20)
      1. When need gives way to greed
      2. When greed leads to corruption
   D. The perils of confiscation (23:5)

III. The making of a righteous, rich man—Note: The general blessing of God makes men rich, the special blessing makes them righteous (11:28)
   A. The richness of righteous living (10:6a)
      1. Security (10:9)
      2. Serenity (10:22b)
      3. Stability (10:25b)
   B. The richness of righteous labor (10:16)
      1. Self-enriching
      2. Others-enriching
   C. The richness of righteous lips (10:21)
      1. Disciplined (10:18–19)
      2. Delightful (10:32)
      3. Discernment (10:13; also 11:13–14; 20–31)
   D. The richness of righteous liberality (11:15–16)
      1. The rightness of caring
      2. The richness of sharing

51

Living Right in a Wicked World

Proverbs 12–13

We are all living in the same world at the same time. But our views of the world and our lifestyles vary greatly. The Bible teaches the world is wicked and we are to live right. But what is necessary to do it?

  I. A clear comprehension of the issues
   A. The condition of a wicked world (1 John 5:19)
   B. The existence of the wicked one (Matt. 13:19)
   C. The reality of a wicked heart (Mark 7:18–23)
   D. The danger of a wicked person (Prov. 15:29; Ps. 19:17)

  II. A clear comprehension of righteousness
   A. The absence of righteous behavior (Ps. 14; Rom. 3:10)
   B. The revelation of righteous requirements (Prov. 13:13)
   C. The advent of the righteous servant (Isa. 53:11)
   D. The possibilities of righteous living (Rom. 8)

III. A careful comparison of the alternatives
   A. Alternative principles
      1. Despising the Word
      2. Fearing the commandments (Prov. 13:13)
   B. Alternative practices
      1. Intentions–straightforward or shady (12:5)
      2. Words–lethal or liberating (12:6)
      3. Attitudes–caring or cruel (12:10)
      4. Desires–fruit or folly (12:12)
      5. Relationships–careful or calculating (12:26)
   C. Alternative prospects
      1. Commendation or condemnation (13:2)
      2. Rooted or rotted (13:3)
      3. Overthrown or overshadowed (13:7)
      4. Sparkling or sputtering (13:9)

IV. A consistent commitment to the Lord involves:
   A. Awareness of right and wrong
   B. Boldness in separating right and wrong
   C. Carefulness in evaluating right or wrong
   D. Decisiveness in choosing right or wrong
   E. Effectiveness in doing right or wrong
   F. Faithfulness in following right or wrong

52

Before Honor Is Humility

Proverbs 14-15

In a society that loves to bestow and receive honors, it is possible that those least deserving are the most highly honored (see Prov. 26:1). To be honored by society is nothing when compared with being honored by God. He spells out the steps to honor.

I. The humility that precedes honor
  A. Attention to God's truth
    1. Understanding how the Lord works (14:2, 31)
    2. Accepting how the Lord evaluates (14:2; 15:16)
    3. Recognizing that the Lord sees (15:3, 11)
    4. Hearing what the Lord says (15:31–32)
    5. Grasping how the Lord feels (15:8–9, 26)
  B. Appraisal of personal status
    1. What am I doing to God? (14:2)
    2. What do I feel about sin? (14:9)
    3. What is the goal of my life? (14:12, 15)
    4. What is really in my heart? (14:13–14)

      5. What is my attitude toward people? (14:21)

      6. What is happening to my soul? (15:32)

  C. Acknowledgment of spiritual failure (14:15–16)

      1. Moral failure is sin

      2. Sin is against God

      3. Sinners humbly seek God's grace
(N.B. Prov. 29:23; 1 Peter 5:5–6)–Beware
of the reaction of the . . .

        a. Willful (Prov. 15:10)

        b. Scornful (15:12)

        c. Wrathful (15:18)

        d. Slothful (15:19)

II. The honor that succeeds humility

  A. On the personal level

      1. Strong confidence (14:26)

        a. Walk (14:2)

        b. Witness (14:25)

        c. Well-being (14:11)

      2. Cheerful countenance (15:13)

        a. A full heart (14:14)

        b. A sound heart (14:30)

        c. A merry heart (12:13)

        d. A wise heart (15:25)

  B. On the social level

      1. Family life

        a. Building up (14:1)

        b. Bursting forth (14:11)

      2. Business life

        a. Industry (14:4)

        b. Investments (14:23)

        c. Insight (15:16–17)

      3. Social life

        a. Being neighborly (14:21)

        b. Being charitable

  C. On the national level (14:34)

53

God and Man

Proverbs 16-17

The Bible does not debate God's existence or argue about his nature. It simply reveals them. It treats man in a similar way and goes on to show the relationship between God and man. Nothing could be more important than an understanding of this subject.

I. Man's recognition of God's majesty
  A. The majesty of his name
    1. *ʾēl*–the ancient name for God
    2. *Yahweh*–the God of Israel
    3. *ʾădōnāy*–the one who has authority
  B. The majesty of his eternal purpose (16:4)
    1. He is the originator of all things
    2. Some things are not as he originated them
    3. He will use all things to bring about his purposes
  C. The majesty of his eternal principles
    1. The principle of authority (16:4)

    2. The principle of integrity (16:11)
    3. The principle of reality (17:3)
    4. The principle of morality (17:15)
  D. The majesty of his eternal power–Note: Man is as free as a fish in water
    1. Power to intervene (16:1)
    2. Power to determine (16:9)
    3. Power to overrule (16:33)

II. Man's response to God's mastery
  A. The response of dedication (16:3)
  B. God purges man's iniquity (16:6)
  C. God handles man's enemies (16:7)
  D. God inspires man's morality (16:11)
  E. God guarantees man's prosperity (16:20)
  F. God controls man's destiny (16:33)
  G. God blesses man's adversity (17:3)

54

The Use of Words

Proverbs 18-19

Words are the chief media of human communication. They can be used to hurt or heal, to harm or help, and accordingly must be used with the greatest care and discernment.

   I. The importance of words
      A. God's unique method of self-revelation
         1. The spoken word–"God said . . ." (Gen. 1)
         2. The living Word (John 1:1; 6:63)
      B. Man's unique method of societal communication
         1. Words as deep waters (Prov. 18:4a)
         2. Wells of divine wisdom (18:4b)
      C. Man's unique method of spiritual application
         1. Take words with you (Hosea 14:2)
         2. Make sure they have meaning (Mal. 2:17)

II. The impact of words
   A. The power to harm
      1. The words of the fool (Prov. 18:6–7)
         a. Strife
         b. Strokes
      2. The words of the gossip (18:8)
         a. Spreading unsubstantiated rumors
         b. Speaking indiscriminate truth
      3. The words of the rash (18:13)
         a. Carelessness (18:2)
         b. Shallowness (18:17)
      4. The words of the liar (19:5, 9)
         a. Contrary to man's best interests
         b. Contrary to God's requirements (19:16)
      5. The words of the nag (19:13)
         a. Demoralizing effect (see also 21:9, 19)
         b. Eroding impact
      6. The tongue of the wicked (19:28)—Note:
         both speaker and hearer get harmed
         (18:20–21)
         a. Relishing wrongness
         b. Regurgitating wickedness
   B. The power to help
      1. The wounded spirit (18:14)
      2. The offended brother (18:19)
      3. The impoverished man (18:23; cf. 19:17)
      4. The discouraged husband (18:22)
      5. The misguided son (19:13, 18, 25)

III. The improvement of words
   A. In terms of material (19:8–12)
   B. In terms of manner (19:23)
   C. In terms of method (Eccles. 3:7)

Cassette tapes of the sermons preached from the outlines in this book are available from

TELLING THE TRUTH
P.O. Box 11
Brookfield, WI 53005